INHERITANCE OF COURAGE AND FEAR

poems by

Anna Mae Perillo

Finishing Line Press
Georgetown, Kentucky

INHERITANCE OF COURAGE AND FEAR

Copyright © 2020 by Anna Mae Perillo
ISBN 978-1-64662-306-8 First Edition
All rights reserved under International and Pan-American Copyright Conventions. No part of this book may be reproduced in any manner whatsoever without written permission from the publisher, except in the case of brief quotations embodied in critical articles and reviews.

ACKNOWLEDGMENTS

"Nest of Worries" was published in *Contrapositions Magazine*, Volume V, 2015.

"Civilized" was inspired by Rousseau's painting "The Sleeping Gypsy". No disrespect is intended to the Romani people by using the term. The facts quoted are from *#resistancegeneology* created by Jennifer Mendelson.

"The Club" was a group of eight women including my mother Mae who held onto each other for as long as they could. Mae passed in 2013 at age 89. The last one standing, Dotty, passed in 2018 at age 97.

A special thank you to my supportive and favorite fans, my husband John and my children Michael and Marlana, and for the encouragement of Carmen, Janice, Lisa, my sisters in IWWG, and my poetry friends in our New York City Workshops.

Publisher: Leah Maines
Editor: Christen Kincaid
Cover Art: Anna Mae Perillo
Author Photo: Nancy Costello Miller
Cover Design: Elizabeth Maines McCleavy

Order online: www.finishinglinepress.com
                  also available on amazon.com

Author inquiries and mail orders:
Finishing Line Press
P. O. Box 1626
Georgetown, Kentucky 40324
U. S. A.

Table of Contents

Putanesca 1

The Numbers of Inheritance 3

For Carmen 7

The Club 9

Haiku for My Mother 11

Mother 12

Mother's Day Special 14

Pity Party 15

Civilized 16

Amelie 18

Nest of Worries 19

Mama Lion or Don't Mess With My Kid 21

I Raised My Children 22

March Madness 23

A Boy Lying Listless Against a Wall on a New York
    City Sidewalk 26

Street Beat 27

Be Here Now 28

To my mother Mae who had a boundless amount of love for her family and an inexhaustible number of mantras, my favorites: "You can do anything you set your mind to," and "Where there's life there's hope."

To my dad, Mayor Vito, who at 96 continues to inspire by example.

PUTANESCA

I don't write about snow, or Christmas, or bunnies.
An occasional   bird may screech by,
as I place a grave blanket   on my mother.
I write about *her* screech.
She wanted to serve day-old spaghetti,
spongy, sticky,
with the sauce we had carefully simmered
with artichoke hearts, capers, tomatoes,
flavors melding   into a "Naughty Lady" recipe.
I begged to contribute   a one-dollar
new box of spaghetti,
and she went
         Crazy.
That's not just an expression—
         Cray-Z

I won't write about trees
painted white with winter,
large flakes of snow, so picturesque.
I will tell you of the chill   inside   arthritic bones,
and memories   of the annual Christmas
tree-chucking,
—out the door—
they were not the right shape
for my mother's liking.

I don't stare into the face of a flower,
looking for inspiration—
I know, shame on me;   I studied the romantics.
Yet, I love a shmaltzy movie
with pink rose petals   strewn
like a map   to loving.
Yet, I name myself "optimistic"—
spoke at my sister's third wedding,
recited the Quran about spouses wearing each other
         like garments,

even though it's difficult to wear a spouse
when we're worn, threadbare, shivering,
instead of heart-warmed—
yet we persevere.

I could write about the ballet academy across the street,
about   young muscles   arabesque-ing,
twirling, dizzy youth. I
was a ballerina once *en pointe*
in pink satin shoes   stuffed at the toe
with lambs' wool to protect them, especially the large
broken toe,
from when I kicked my high school love
who called me   "whore",
in between presenting me with gifts of gems and Led Zeppelin tickets.
Balancing then, on top of our seats in silver platform shoes.
I was   heart-crushed,
when I lost my *Sleeping Beauty* lead   because of that crushed toe.
So, I won't write about the ballerinas I see
practicing in their pink leotards.
I look away, but not before
hoping, for each of them—
that one day, they will pirouette   across a city street,
with large snowflakes fluttering down   like rose petals,
and fall   right into the arms
of a deserving love.

THE NUMBERS OF INHERITANCE

I.

My father was all over the news this week!
Local, national even international with large regal photos,
and interviews in our family home where he lives
alone   among the looming silk flower arrangements,
angel statues, marble David and turquoise Botticelli lamps—
my late mother's touches.
        New York Times
               Seattle Times
                     Rome and Amsterdam
Times:
November 7, 2017, a 93-year-old, World War II veteran,
                            never before held public office,
Mayor-elect of Tinton Falls, New Jersey.

As the results rolled in,
he looked stoic.
We, his family, erupted in cheers—
"Oh my God, you won!" we shouted with   astonishment,
unbelieving pride.
Me, then, as tears surged   trying to look   composed,
placed my hand on his shoulder for photos,
in between his recounting—
walking door to door, two pairs of shoes   disintegrating,
like memories of an old man he didn't want to become.

"How does it feel to be a 93-year-old mayor?"
the reporters queried over and over.
"It's like any other day," he repeated.
"Like when you're 41 and turn 42, you're the same   person . . . .
I want to get past all that, get to my new job."
I wanted to   holler when they panned on his news-
worthy hands. He did not want the attention,
no less, because of his age.

II

My grandmother, my mother's mother,
had forget-me-not eyes,
soft curls in black hair, she was all   roundness and comfort.
Nylons rolled down swollen legs
I called "eggs" at 2, when I offered to rub them.
She was always ready,
with a packed suitcase, a friendly wave
as she periodically went off   to the hospital.
Always ready,
with a hard candy, or Blackjack Gum   for her insulin-induced
sugar dips, or a treat for her grandchildren.
Only *her* candies melted in my mouth.
Only *her* gum made me laugh   when we stuck out our tongues
to marvel   at their black-licorice color.
She died at 59,
when I was 6.

Only 6—
including some unremembering
baby years, but I have   decades
of memories   of being her granddaughter—
a liked child. Big, safe years.
she was amused by my spunky tongue
when I said, with hands on my hips, at 3,
"I'll do what I want, when I want, and how I wanna do it."
She let me hide behind her abundant hips
clothed in floral cotton dresses;
it was like being in a   spring garden,
as my mother tried to "get me".
When my mother calmed down, my grandmother laughed,
gestured with her hand—
fingers close together, waived briskly up and down, meaning:
"You have a pip on your hands."

"You inherited your love of books from her," my mother often said.
Trying to   impress her   at 4,
I pretended to read small-print,
grown-up books,
secretly counting the letters.

Her photo sits in our living rooms
in gold gilded frames.
We spend time with her that way,
her no-anger eyes   following us.

III

My mother was dying for 30 years,
after turning 59,
figuring,   she had inherited death.
Amazed when she turned 60, then 70, then 80—
she'd lift her hands toward me, palms down, and say,
"See? These are old hands."
They were, and at 89 on her hospice death-bed,
we held them one more time.

This week   in a dream   I was overwhelmed   by a body of water
I had to traverse in the dark.
Relieved when another who went before me,
touched her feet to sand   beneath the murky treachery.
When I awoke, my mother visiting my mind said,
"Dreaming of water, especially dark water, means troubles, honey."
I argued: "But if I was able to walk through it, isn't that hopeful?"
She just shook her head,
"No. That's not good,"
and left me again.

IV

I won't let my family throw me
milestone birthdays. I won't
even say   which milestones. My hands are starting to look
like my mother's when she found them   betraying.
(I don't show them to my daughter.)
I use them to thrash   black   angry water,
tread with wild strokes.
Any time it reaches my chin,
I thrust my head back   ungracefully,
crane my nostrils toward the sky,
breath the salt air.

I'm left,
caught between my inheritances—
with my book-holding hands,
reading   about strength   and courage
in a corner, with the shades drawn,
against a new year passing,
because, you see,
I have also inherited fear.

FOR CARMEN

If I were working in clay,
I would take my fingertips,
smooth the lines around your mouth, the creases
between your eyebrows.
My sculpture would be   young,
like when we met in front of a bulletin board
amid the jumble of notices—rooms and apartments to rent
for our junior year in college. Then,
strangers living together.

Skeptical, but absorbent like sponges,
we searched for truth in our textbooks and lectures.
You in a box, speaking French—
Existentialist theatre, they called it.
My poetry classes held in professors' living rooms—
Wine and cheese—we were   oh   so   sophisticated.
Instead of parent furniture, they had decorative floor cushions
we'd sit on, cross-legged, like we were ready to meditate.
(These professors knew what was happening!)

If I could name the play, speaker and context of
every Shakespeare quote,
didn't that mean I was educated?
And if you could take those numbers and do whatever the
hell you were doing with them,
    (even if you slept through a few exams)
weren't you ready?

We have computers now,
houses and portfolios,
couches and curios,
        (We didn't find floor-cushions practical.)
children and china   counting on steady hands.
It calls for   a graceful dance—

Afro-Caribbean Movements had surely prepared us for this.
Marriage counselors and merry-go-rounds,
business cards and babies,
in-laws and in-line skating,
husbands,
    husbands and children,
        husbands and children and our thriving businesses.

Did you hear Avon is making a new night cream? The promise
of alpha hydroxy.
And Clairol Loving Care washes away the gray, premature of course.

We are educated.
We have advanced degrees   in multi-colored frames,
but do you remember how proud we were
of our wall-hanging of the rams?
We were self-sufficient, particularly in the snow—
provisions of salt, shovel, cans of tuna   thrown in the backseat.
We would not be stranded again, like we were that time at the frat
with men who growled like lions, vomited,
and then ate fried eggs.

We would not be stranded.
    We could shovel ourselves out of a drift.

THE CLUB

When Betty started dying,
They started going to the movies.
They needed the dark,
The even rows of seats and to feel each other's shoulders,
Share popcorn and jujubes,
And images of other people dying or laughing.

Eight women, then seven, then six,
And now Betty.
Their living rooms filled with chips and ginger ale
Were too large. Their talk of the Turkey Farm outing,
The Club's Christmas dinner, new Weight Watchers food
Was too small, because Betty only weighed 95 pounds now,
Like she always dreamed.

Friends for 30 years by that time,
They remembered when most of them still had slender thighs,
And their little daughters played dress-up and produced garage plays.
Helen's husband turned out to be a bum—
Left her pregnant with her third child.
Savanah's last child born imperfect,
Well, they moved to Florida.

They sought no acupuncture, yoga or gestalt,
Didn't turn to vodka or too many pills,
Every other Thursday
Women and cake,
Coffee and confessions,
Conversation to last two more weeks.

After Betty died, her mother came to the meeting
With a box of scarves, earrings, belts, and sweater tops.
Betty had been a sharp dresser.
"Pass the chips and dip.
Look at that red sweater; it would look perfect on you!"

Mae said, "It wouldn't fit over one of my basooms!"
They all roared. And looking up,
"Betty, you made us laugh again!"
Big Doris wrapped a pair of red beads around her neck.
Dotty tried on the black hoop earrings.
Mae draped the poppy orange scarf around her neck
Letting it fall gracefully over her large chest.
Caroline tried on a purple tunic with gold embroidery,
Helen an aqua knit vest.

"Jess is having bypass next week."
"My daughter's divorce goes through tomorrow."
"She's better off; Jess will be too," they chattered.

When Helen's daughter Patti, at 40,
Suffered the unthinkable—
Lost her leg and hip to cancer at Sloane Kettering,
The "girls" went to the Chinese Buffet.
Fried Dumplings, greasy ribs, General Tso's chicken, chocolate soft serve
Was what they needed. And then,
They gathered around Patti's bed
In the tiny room she had grown up in,
Offered up small talk and words of praise,
"Look at her healthy round cheeks and soulful eyes.
You are so pretty, Patti!"

When Patti joined Betty,
Mae picked up Dotty and Big Doris, Caroline, and Helen,
Their hair carefully combed; rosy shades of lipstick brightening their faces.
They giggled when Dotty couldn't get the seatbelt around her waist,
And when Doris had to be pushed out of the backseat.
They all needed an outing,
Because their living rooms were too empty;
Their lost friends   hung like images in a holographic museum,
So real, they might believe they could reach out to touch them,
But they could not be held.

HAIKU FOR MY MOTHER

Her tears trickle down—
stiff stooped angry fist raised high;
she is old today.

MOTHER

My Mother was like the month of March—
In like a lion,
Out like a lamb.
My aunt says when they were children,
"Mae was a bully."
When she caught her jumping over the johnny pumps,
Unladylike for their father's daughters, forbidden,
She said to her sister,
"You tell Daddy, I'll pull out every hair on your head."

Have you heard the expression,
    "crack him over the head with a frying pan"?
My mother did that,
Only it wasn't always a frying pan;
It could be a milk pitcher, tea cup, whatever was handy.
She counselled my sister and me about husbands, or maybe
People in general,
"You have to fight, or they'll bury you."

Before the expression, "road rage" was coined,
Several times, my mother walked right up to another driver's window,
Unhappy about some maneuver.
Holding pencil and paper, she'd say,
"Let me see your license; I'm making a citizen's arrest."

The thing that pissed her off more than anything
Was getting older.
She'd raise her fist at the sky,
"God damn it," she'd bellow,
"Old age is a bitch!"

She spoke of her own feared death often.
If she was mad at someone,
She'd warn, "If she comes to the funeral home,
I'll sit straight up from the casket and spit right in her eye."

At about age 87, still ready to engage in battle
Over pot roast or meatballs up to this point,
She began to appear more serene, smiling warmly,
Delighted to have some hungry mouths to feed.
It took me a while to figure out—
She had begun leaving her hearing aids somewhere other
Than in her ears, and admitted when confronted,
She was happier that way.

In the hospital, she refused my offer of TV,
As she held hands with the man she had fought for 64 years,
"We don't need TV; we talk all night and give each other kisses."
"What the hell!" my sister and I said,
"Why couldn't we have grown up with this?"

On her deathbed, she was a calm, warm breeze.
She was the end of March,
Telling us she would miss us all. Calling me
Her "movie star". She whispered,
I should make my sister help me with Christmas dinner,
And teach my father how to wash the escarole—my least favorite task.
She held our hands, smiled, and closed her eyes.

(By the way, she was peaceful at the funeral home too; there was no spitting.)

MOTHER'S DAY SPECIAL

She was just trying to sell
little chocolate nibs   five flavors,
at the health food store—
natural with just a smattering of chemicals.

Her job—to encourage one to sample.
At once personable and pushy,
insistent   I try all five flavors,
five times the price of drug-store candy.

Me, usually friendly, just wanted to buy my vitamins,
tried to move along.
 "Mothers and chocolate always go together," she said.
I answered snappily, "My mother is dead."
She said, "Mine is too."

PITY PARTY

I count my losses
like, ungratefully,
counting coins.

We ought to have a day!
To gather,
recall our sorrows, deficits—
a more expansive Memorial Day,
less patriotic.
Or is that unnecessary since we have
Prozac and medicinal marijuana?
Or is that Saturday night with a bottle of vodka?
Or should we be content with individual vigils—
lighting a candle,
as if a flame does not recall hell.

The ghosts haunt my dreams.
One has the face of my mother.
I would be better off   holding their hands,
but I fight them,
unaccepting.

Cannot decide if those who have vanished,
are more concerning   than those left here   struggling,
looking up at the sky   for comfort   for hope
counting each day,
as if it were a blessing.

CIVILIZED
(A poem in two voices)

Even an untamed lion sniffing
At the back of the coal-colored gypsy
Did not devour her,
Did not drink from her jar of clean water.
Overcome by fatigue, she sleeps
On the cold sandy ground   next to her mandolin.

    "You cannot rebuild civilization with somebody else's babies,"
        the U.S. Congressman said in 2017.
    Aren't we all somebody else's babies?
    Who said we're rebuilding civilization?
    Resistancegeneology revealed this congressman's grandmother
    immigrated from Germany at four,
    holding her two-year old brother's hand, clutching
    her baby sister, afraid
    of being devoured   by newness   by denial.

I stumble across the Sleeping Gypsy,
Sit beside her
On the other side from where the lion stands.
I hope he will allow my humble intrusion,
Needing to rest, myself.
I gently strum the mandolin,
Trying to remember a lullaby.

    The Director of Social Media railed against "chain migration",
    as if flesh and blood created a metal fence, and
    not an American family
    living together in New York like
    his family. His great-grandfather Victor arrived in 1904,
    Victor's brothers in 1905 and 1912, his sister in 1913,
    another sister and his father in 1916—
    linked.
    Sepia toned photos in boxes in basements
    brought out, scattered on kitchen tables as each relative passes.
    Chain linked.
    Fenced in only by the unaccepting groups who got here
    before   it became cool to eat "pasta" and fly to Tuscany
    for vacation.

I cover the young woman with my soft, blue shawl
Woven from tears and well-wishes,
And pray to Elpis, goddess of hope.

> The twenty-five-year old, "white-power Barbie"
> commentator for Fox News and the Great
> American Alliance,
> prattled, "Dreamers and their families are
> not law-abiding."
> "No comment," when confronted with proof that her
> great-grandfather was indicted by a grand jury—
> forged his naturalization papers.

The young gypsy continues to sleep.
She dreams tomorrow she will find her sister and mother.
They will make a home for themselves
And for her father   who works with metal,
His hands cut   and calloused.
She does not know I'm with her,
Imagining the music her family will create together—
The hollow, holy sound of the bamboo pan flute,
The haunting notes of the cimbalom,
Mixed with the sweetness   of her strings.
It's the least I can do—align
With the lion,
And fight the fear of being devoured myself.

AMELIE

I was told my baby might be dying inside of me.
My friend Catarina said she would knit for me,
Blankets of the softest cotton yarns,
In yellows and golds—
For a child who would be like royalty to us.

My friend Marina said she would pray nightly,
Caressing her shiny silver beads,
Decades upon decades,
Hail Mary's, asking the Blessed Mother to intercede. Our Fathers—
For a child who would be like an angel to us.

My friend Nadia said she would think beautiful thoughts,
As she cleaned and polished, scrubbed and mopped,
With each motion,
With each drop of sweat, an offering—
For a child who would be a servant of joy to our hearts.

My friend Maya said she would light incense
At her dresser alter with her turquoise Buddha, hand carved cross,
Picture of her late mother, and a piece of coral
From a sacred beach in Indonesia—
For a child who would be a dancer on the sands of our own shore.

It could have gone another way.
Weeks went by, and when the pains started,
My friends gathered around my bed
With yarn, beads, incense and clean cloths.
The child and I struggled and strained
Until my friends   held her up,
With exaltation, with gratitude,
Welcoming a new daughter
Who would be allowed to walk this earth,
And would belong   to all of us.

NEST OF WORRIES

In the daytime I seem fine,
But at night
I am a weaver,
A weaver and a builder.
One by one
        Jagged twigs
        Dried grass
I form an egg-shaped hollow
My widening behind   can plop right into—
My nest of worries.

My daughter, my small girl lost   on a city street,
Some low-life mother-fucker hollering
With a gesture   involving his hand   and tongue
        He can kiss my ass!
She is beautiful—delicate frame, oval doe eyes—
Exotic they say.

Her father, my husband
A mad man,
Pulling out his hair
Throwing plates down a courthouse hallway—
        And Justice for All.
His kidney stones pressing through his scalp,
He shakes his head from side to side   like trying to rid his ears   of
Pool water.
When I met him at twenty-three, he said   he could not wait
To turn sixty.

My son, my boy, my man, on a plane looking
For a job, a school, a girl, a drink . . .
He had hundred-dollar bills cramming his wallet,
But by the time he lands, there is no money left.

One of their grandparents cannot walk, one cannot breathe,
One has cancer, dementia—cannot remember my children's names.
We are glad to have them, but wish
Sometimes, they could take care of us again.

My clients are all getting divorced,
That is no surprise.
It's what I do: hold hands, keep them from grabbing each other
By the throat.
Don't use the word "fair" I counsel,
Say "acceptable".
For after all, that is what we can hope for—
A life that is acceptable.

In the daytime I seem fine,
But at night
I am a weaver,
A weaver and a builder   of my beautiful
Nest of worries.

MAMA LION or DON'T MESS WITH MY KID

You can't shut *me* up.
Don't try to cover *my* mouth.
I'll scream, spit, claw, chew   bite!
So, keep it up,
Keep it coming, baby.

Your swollen, sweating hands reach up and over,
Pinning a child against a cinderblock school wall.
The hideousness of your insides
Reek of rotted flesh.
You need to air yourself out, inside out.

I can pound *my* fists too.
I can speak with spittle flying   out of *my* mouth too.
I can raise *my* arms too, but when I do
It will be to wave them like a flag of glory,
While running   a lap of victory.

I'm almost done with you. Your lashes will leave welts,
But I will wear them like a badge   with my chest puffed out,
Or like a metal helmet, prepared for anyone else
Who wants to attempt a head-bashing.

I RAISED MY CHILDREN

I raised my children
to be like field sparrows—
free, but busy and disciplined.

I raised my children
with the luck   of my moonstone,
rubbed with worry.

I raised my children
to fly off   like Red Admiral Butterflies—
to stand out, but humbly.

I raised my daughter
to be strong like Sekhmet, the lioness goddess.
My son like Horus, lord of the sky.
They fly around the world to places
I can't find on a map   like Heliopolis and Valhalla.

I raised my children
to connect their past to the future,
to walk on a suspension bridge
slowly, more like the tortoise   than the hare.

I raised my children
to be flavorful   like Sweetheart cherries,
a treat for the senses.

I raised my children
not to be common, grocery-store apples,
but to be pomegranates.

I raised my children
to know my favorite color is magenta,
the color I think of
when I feel them   in my heart.

MARCH MADNESS

In March, I shrink and plummet   deep down
into the still chilled earth's core,
unable to join in the jubilee—
celebrations with bunnies and bonnets.
As basketball fans exuberate,
I sink into   my own madness.

I periodically glance   out my kitchen window in March.
Observe the goings-on out there:
the crocuses poke up, scattered about the lawn
like cool teenagers, with tufts of pink and purple hair.

        Maybe I should dye *my* hair.

The snow drops announce themselves   defiantly,
slicing through the icy residue, then
dancing gracefully   in frequent   stiff winds.

        I play rhythmic music, try to *dance* myself happier.

The green stems of the daffodil bulbs
raise their hands like classroom children
wanting to be polite, but causing a clamor.

        Maybe I should go back to teaching; surround myself
        with youth.

One day, the pushy pink flowers of the redbud tree,
too impatient to await leaves, appear
straight out of brown branches.

        "We're getting there," people say to each other,
        myself   included, but I'm losing patience.

March plays cat and mouse here in the northeast,
teasing with alternate warmth and chill.
I appreciate the small glimmers, loveliness springing up,
but we can't put our boots away.

I suspect it's not just the weather, though, so I ask:
Is it like New Years' Eve with that pressure to feel elated?
Is it my resistance to ageing?
Fear and dread passed on   by my mother.
March *is*   my birthday month.

I resist the invitation to move winter's wall away,
to embrace new energy, better-angled light.
I'm still thawing   inside,
with fireplaces, stews, and hot steeped teas.

When I go out, I enjoy sitting in a car   left in the sun—
a reminder of what is not yet here, but of what will come.
A reminder, that in summer, my mood will lift.
I close my eyes   as the car window refracts sunlight.
The left side of my face and my denim-clad thighs   begin to warm.

I close my eyes   and envision summer scenes:

Yo yo yo!
I see you   with your cosmos   and coronas with limes   peeking
out of their bottle necks. Clams on the grill
their shells opening   like smiles,
with lemon, with butter!

Yo yo yo!
I see you too—
me afraid to wear a black one-piece,
you   bounding down the beach   in your bikini with
even more belly than I have,
wearing it proudly.
I applaud you!   I admire you!

I picture myself   with my blanket   and books,
watching toddlers playing tag   with the white foam of the surf,
until their high-pitched voices require headphones.

Yo yo yo!
I'm listening to Yo   Yo
*   Ma*
My head swaying to the singular notes of his cello.

You see? I am being cheered already!

In March   I am a dormant bulb.
I bide my time until I'm ready
to claw   up   through   the dense   soil
to meet   the sun.

A BOY LYING LISTLESS AGAINST A WALL ON A NEW YORK CITY SIDEWALK

He was about thirteen
with course, ruddy-blond hair, so unlike
the almost-black   polished hair   of my own children.
I sensed immediately, he needed   something.
In my gut I knew it wasn't Narcan.

(No planning, no 911)
I cradled his head
felt the dull muted strands   with my cupped hand,
guided him   to my breast,
willing mind over matter
after so many years,

waited   for the letting down,
the invited mother-tingling,
to conjure a drink
for the cracked lips
of someone else's child.

STREET BEAT

I had just commented
on our way to dinner
how sorry I felt for the homeless   in this
freezing cold, before the wind
whipped us around the corner   and
      there he was, a homeless man,
in a stadium chair,   his throne.
Bright blanket   over his legs
red ski cap   perched   like a crown.
"Viva la France!" he cheered. Then he began to chant
"Clickety clack, clickety clack . . ."
And I realized his rhythm
mirrored   the tap tapping   of my black suede boots.
"There she goes, Miss Clickety Clack!"

Indictment?   Admiration?   I
felt the truth of   all of it.
Allowing myself a brief   respite
from the week's teeth gnashing and impudence,
strutting   in my new Cole Haan coat, Michael Kors purse
on the arm   of my handsome son,

And the shame of it   too—
here I was,   in the city,   looking for poetry,
and finding   a poet   hearing rhythm
and seeing   who   I   am:
Miss Clickety Clack.

BE HERE NOW

This is what we have:
Two eyelids blinking   one time.

A sip of iced tea.

Feeling the softness   of worn denim   caressing thighs.

Locking eyes for one second   with a stranger.

The tart taste   of the first bite   of a Fuji apple.

The movement of teeth and jaw   eating one   unsalted   cashew.

Reading one word at a time—
   yellowing pages filling nostalgic nostrils,
So then:
         one image of a favorite library   in an old house,
and then:
         sitting on a couch   with a colorful stack of books,
or:
         lying stretched out on the floor
            reading in front of a bay window   behind heavy curtains,
         a flash of lightening
            making a Nancy Drew mystery   more mysterious.

One frame   of a movie.

One note   of the cello.

The first glimpse of cityscape—
   buildings clustered   in geometric form.

One drop of sweat   forming on a forehead,

One cool breeze   refreshing.

One wave splashing   against the ferry dock.

The spire of the Chrysler building
    directing we stand taller   this one time.

This is what we have:
One beam of sunlight.

One bee alighting   on a yellow flower.

This one   hug.

One wag   of a dog's brown tail.

Feeling an earring   dangle,

A glimpse   in the mirror,

This one stroke   of my hand   over your forehead.

And one second from now: more.
And one minute from now: even   more.

ANNA MAE PERILLO is a poet, novelist and playwright who writes at the Jersey Shore, in New York City and just about anywhere else her voice and the voices of others, including her ancestors, command she take notice. She has recently completed her first novel, *Porcelain* and her second short play, *Mariana & the Wild Boars,* which has been accepted for production by the Manhattan Repertory Theatre. She earned a bachelor's degree in English & Education, minor in Dance from Rutgers University and a Juris Doctorate from Seton Hall University. Anna Mae has taught as an adjunct faculty member in the Writing Department at Brookdale Community College and practices law in Red Bank, New Jersey primarily as a divorce mediator. As a pioneer of peaceful resolution, she teaches mediation skills to other professionals. Anna Mae has given poetry readings in New York City, Miami, and in a digital global village as a member of the International Women's Writing Guild.

www.ingramcontent.com/pod-product-compliance
Lightning Source LLC
LaVergne TN
LVHW041507070426
835507LV00012B/1383